Written by Odile Limousin
Illustrated by Agnes Mathieu

*Specialist adviser:
Dr Peter Wood,
Technical Executive, RHM Centre*

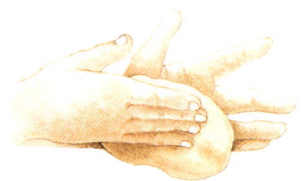

*ISBN 1 85103 135 9
First published 1991 in the United Kingdom
by Moonlight Publishing Ltd,
36 Stratford Road, London W8
Translated by Sarah Gibson*

*© 1985 by Editions Gallimard
English text © 1991 by Moonlight Publishing Ltd
Typeset by Saxon Printing Ltd, Derby
Printed in Italy by Editoriale Libraria*

POCKET • WORLDS

Bread
Around the World

We eat bread every day.
Have you ever wondered
how it's made?

THE WORLD OF FOOD

In Tunisia in North Africa, bread is baked to a dark golden colour, with a hard crust. It will keep for a long time.

There are many different kinds of 'black' bread in Germany; they are made from a mixture of wheat and rye flour.

In India, one of the main foods is a flat bread called a chapatti, baked on a metal plate.

Nothing tastes quite like
freshly baked bread! Crusty
and warm, it's very tempting
to pull off a piece and
tuck in!

**Bread comes in all sorts
of shapes and forms, and
people throughout the
world have been eating it
for thousands of years.**
It is one of our basic foods:
it is filling, and contains
many of the ingredients we
need for a healthy diet.

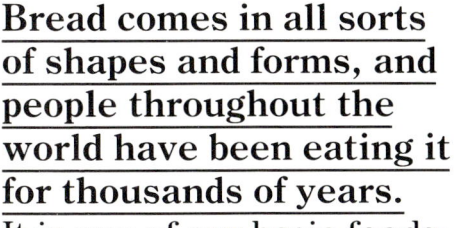

What exactly is bread?
It starts off as a mixture of flour, salt, yeast
and water; this is dough and it has to be
cooked. Sometimes it is more like a flat
cake; the first types of bread were like
this. It was the Egyptians who discovered
that if they left the dough for a while, it
would puff up and so would be a much
lighter bread after it had been baked.
This is 'leavened' bread, and it is the
kind we most often eat in the
West today.

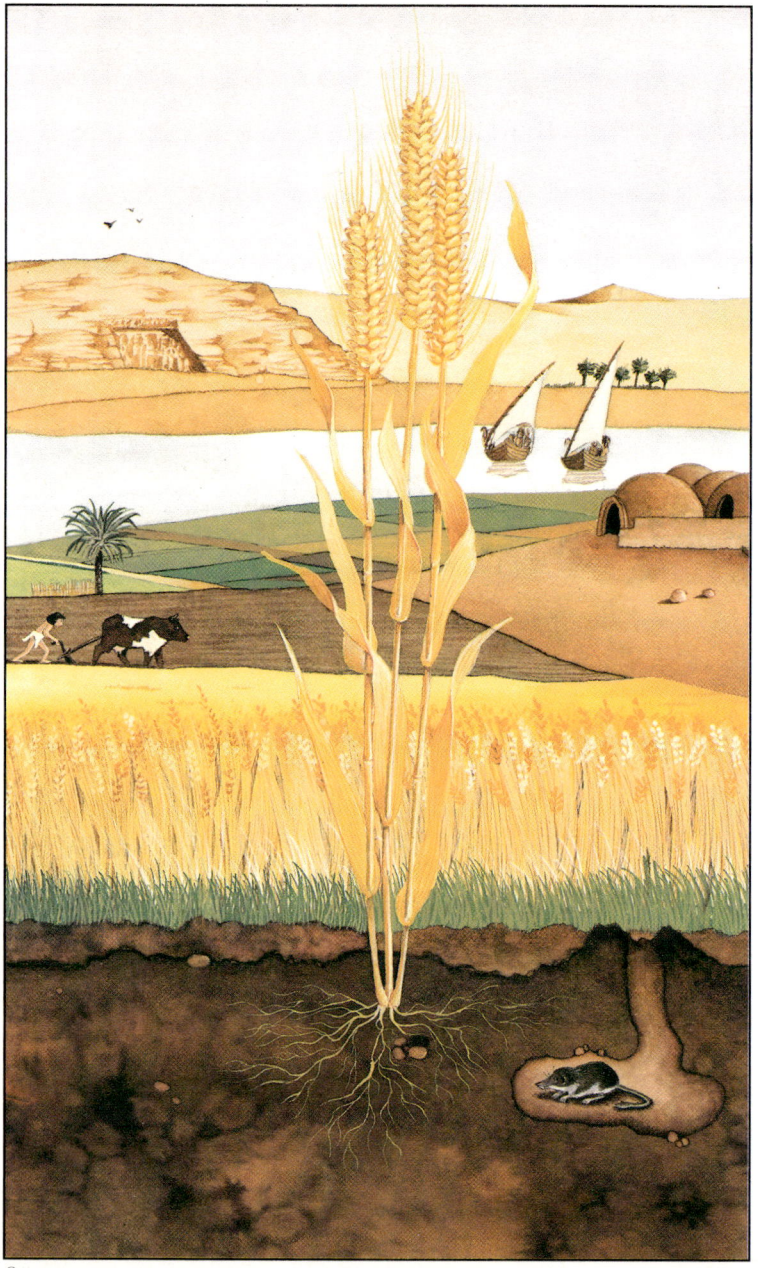

Each type of wheat has a different head of grain; some are bearded, with long, coarse whiskers, some are not.

What is flour made from?

It is nearly always made from grains of a cereal crop. Wheat, like rye, maize or rice, is a type of cereal: a plant which bears a head of grain on each stem. The grain can be ground down to make flour. Wheat flour is the kind we use most often in the West for our bread. **Wholemeal** flour contains the whole of the wheat grain, **white** flour has been refined, with most of the wheat germ and husk sifted out. Both kinds of bread are good for us, but wholemeal is better.

A grain of wheat cut through to show the seed.

A grain of wheat is the same shape as a split almond. The seed, or germ, is at the bottom, and the whole grain is protected by a husk round the outside.

Wheat is grown in large fields. It looks rather like green grass in spring, before it grows tall

and turns golden by midsummer. In the old days, people relied on the harvest to provide enough food for the year. If the crop failed, they might go hungry or starve.

How does wheat grow?

The field is ploughed up, and a harrow breaks up the clods of earth and makes the soil lighter. Now it is ready for seeding. Long ago, the farm labourers scattered the seed by hand. Now farmers use an automatic seed-drill, and a roller to press the seeds into the soil.

Down underground, the seed begins to develop, feeding off the grain at first. Gradually it changes into a little green shoot, with roots that feed from the soil.

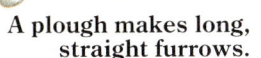

◀ Old-fashioned horse-drawn plough

A plough makes long, straight furrows.

Stems of wheat can be woven into 'corn dollies'. They used to be dried and hung around the farmhouse to bring good luck.

The wheat grows tall and ripens to gold; each stem has a heavy head of grain.

Now it's harvest time!

Even today, in countries where there are few machines, wheat is harvested by hand. It is cut with a sickle, a tool with a short handle and a curved blade, and then it is tied into bundles called sheaves.

The tiny harvest mouse makes her nest in the middle of the corn stalks.

The whole village helps to get the job done before the dry weather breaks, and then it's time to celebrate, with dancing, singing, and a special harvest supper!

Two old-fashioned ways of separating the grain from the husks: here, oxen walk in a circle, trampling on the stalks.

After the wheat is harvested

Each ear of wheat is made up of forty to sixty grains.

The grains have to be separated from the ears and stalks, which can be set aside as straw and used to feed the animals in winter.

Here, the stalks are threshed, or beaten, with long, jointed rods called flails.

A **threshing-machine** driven by steam was invented about 150 years ago. What a difference it made to the farmers! They fed the sheaves into the top, and the grain was separated from the straw. The grain was collected in coarse cloth sacks, and stored in large barns, called granaries.

A modern combine-harvester can harvest a whole field in a single day! It drives slowly up and down, and giant blades gather in the wheat at the front. Inside, the grain is sorted from the straw.

The straw drops out behind, and when the machine is full, the grain pours out of a feeder into a waiting trailer. It is taken to a grain store or a silo, where it can be kept for several years.

How is the grain milled to turn it into flour?

For a long time, grain was simply crushed between two stones. Then the ancient Egyptians and Greeks started to use a club-shaped tool called a pestle to grind the grain in a stone basin called a mortar.

In parts of Asia and in Yemen, millet is still crushed by hand between two stones.

From the millstone to the mill

In Roman bakehouses, slaves were made to crush the grain by turning heavy millstones. Later, mills were built by rivers. In a water-mill, the force of falling water turns a wheel that turns the millstones.

Milling grain in ancient Rome

The Romans invented the water-mill, but windmills came from Palestine.

In the Middle Ages, knights returning to Europe from the Crusades brought the idea back with them. It was very useful for people who lived far from a river! A windmill is usually built on a hilltop. It has two or four sails, which need to be turned so they face the wind. The wind drives the sails round. Some windmills are squat, stone towers, and only the cap carrying the sails turns. Others are small and light, mounted on a post so that the whole mill revolves.

An early windmill

A Greek windmill

Nowadays, grain is usually milled in modern flour-mills which are fully automatic and run on electricity.

Windmill in Afghanistan: it turns on a vertical shaft.

The baker weighs each ball of dough to make sure the loaves of bread are the same weight, then he puts them in a basket.

The baker works all night long,

so that in the morning there's hot, fresh bread ready to sell. He mixes the flour with water, salt, and a special raising agent called **yeast**, to make a firm dough.

He marks the dough with a knife. Can you see the holes left by the bubbles of gas while the bread was baking?

In the old days, the baker had to **knead** the dough by hand. It was very hard work. Nowadays it is mixed in an electric kneading machine. Next it is shaped and left in a warm place for several hours. The yeast gives off tiny bubbles of carbon dioxide gas, which make the dough rise.

This loaf, from Burgundy in France, has been specially decorated for the harvest festival.

When the balls of dough have risen and doubled in size, the baker lifts each one into the oven with a **peel**, rather like a long wooden shovel.
The loaves have to bake for 40 to 60 minutes, depending on their size.

The heat of the oven makes the outside of the bread go crusty. When it comes out, the most delicious smell wafts through the bakery! But we eat far less bread now than we did fifty years ago.

Guess who ate the first sandwich?

It was an English nobleman, Lord Sandwich, of course! He was a very keen card player, and one day in 1762 the game was so exciting that he refused to leave it for dinner. His servants brought him a piece of meat in between two slices of bread; the first sandwich had been invented!

The sliced bread you buy in supermarkets is usually baked in an industrial bakery.

In Morocco, flat unleavened bread is baked on hot metal plates.

For hundreds of years, before ovens were invented, bread was cooked outdoors, over an open fire. It still is, even today, in certain parts of the world: the dough is cooked in a container made of clay or metal, heated on the embers of a fire.
In some countries it's fried in hot oil, like a fritter or a doughnut.

The invention of the bread oven was a huge step forward. The Greeks were the first to think of this method.

In Afghanistan, bread is sometimes made in a cooking-pot.

In Iran, little squares of bread dough are fried in oil.

The traditional bread oven was dome-shaped, and built outdoors from bricks, earth or stones. By the end of the 19th century, coal replaced wood as fuel, and finally steam or electricity was used.
The bakers of ancient Greece had other good ideas: they sweetened their bread with honey and raisins, and they also discovered that if a piece of bread was baked twice, it went crisp. It was popular: they had invented the biscuit!

Families took turns to bake their bread in a shared oven. In some countries, this still happens.

The bakers of Athens used to make sixty-two different sorts of bread. Every country in the world, and almost every region, has its own speciality. Have you eaten pitta bread from Greece, a Scottish barley bannock, or a baguette from France? Look at all the different shaped breads we can eat!

White bread

Cob or Coburg loaf

Bloomer

Austrian baguette

French baguette

Bread sticks

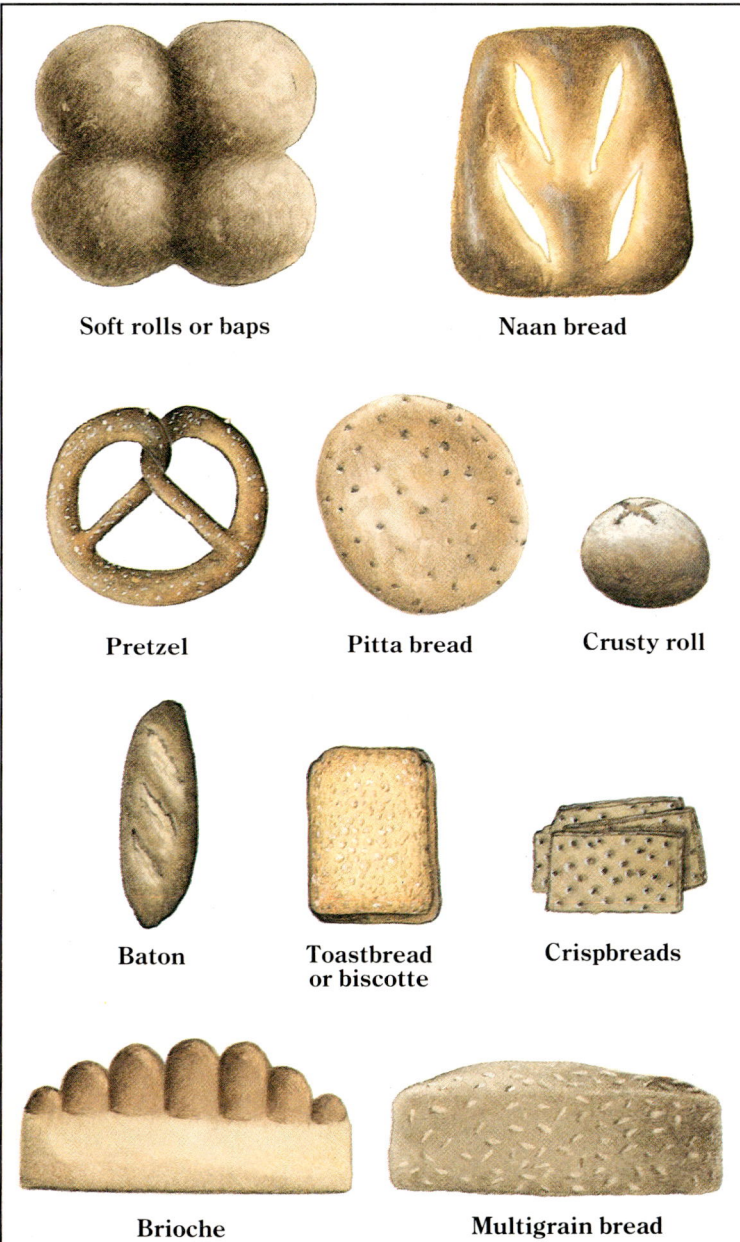

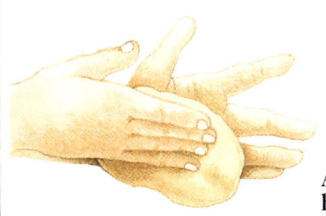

A tortilla is shaped between the hands before it is baked.

People all over South America, Africa and the Middle East eat different types of unleavened bread.

It does not have yeast to make it rise, so it is flat like a thick pancake. It can be made from wheat, or millet, or maize. In Mexico, people make it with maize, and call it tortilla. They eat it with almost all their dishes. In Africa, millet is more often used. Bread can be made from other cereals, too. Rye grows in cooler climates and makes a dark brown bread, with a strong, nutty flavour. You find it in Eastern Europe and Scandinavia.

Wheat   Millet   Oats   Rye   Barley   Maize

In many countries round the Mediterranean, a special sweet bread almost like a cake is made at Easter time. It is decorated with a red painted egg.

In Yugoslavia, if a boy is in love with a girl, he may give her a little heart made of bread.

Bread baked on festival days in Egypt has a decoration stamped on it: a custom that dates back to the Pharaohs!

In Japan, bread is baked in different shapes for people to take home with them after a pilgrimage, or for New Year.

In many countries, special bread is baked for special occasions. Some is crisp like a biscuit, some is soft and spongy.

Chinese New Year Bread

Do you know these expressions?

A baker's dozen: 13!
Bakers used to be fined if their bread weighed light, so they would put 13 loaves in a batch of a dozen just to be sure.

New Year Pretzel from Germany

She knows which side her bread is buttered!
She knows how to act in her own best interests!

Festive Breton bread

On the breadline:
with only just enough money to buy food.

Easter Plait

The bread winner:
The wage earner.

Pilgrim bread

To want your cake and eat it too:
To want everything your own way.

Yugoslavian Christmas bread

Try making bread shapes of your own!

You can buy bread dough mix in a packet. Add water, follow the instructions and you've got dough ready to model with! You can use currants for eyes, and a little beaten egg to brush over the top.

Put the dough on a floured board, and pinch off small pieces to model with, or press shapes out with pastry cutters. Here are some ideas for you, but you can make up your own. They will need to bake in a hot oven (200°C, Gas Regulo 6) for 20 to 30 minutes, depending on their size. Have fun!

Index

baking, 23-5
barley bannock, 28
biscuit, invention of, 27
black bread, 6
bread oven, 25-7
cereal, 9, 31
chapatti, 6, 31
combine-harvester, 16
corn dollies, 13
dough, 7, 23, 25, 26, 34
doughnut, 26
Egyptian bread-making, 7, 18
festive breads, 32-3

flour, 7, 9
food value of bread, 7
French baguette, 28
granary, 15
Greek bread-making, 18, 26, 27, 28
harrow, 11
harvest, 11, 13
harvest festival, 13, 23
harvest mouse, 13
harvest supper, 13
husk, 9, 14
kneading, 23
leavened bread, 7

maize, 9, 31
millet, 18, 31
milling, 18, 21
millstones, 18
peel, 25
pestle and mortar, 18
pitta bread, 28
planting seed, 11
plough, 11
pretzel, 33
Roman bread-making, 18
rye, 6, 31
sandwich, 25

sickle, 13
silo, 17
sliced bread, 25
threshing, 14-15
tortilla, 31
unleavened bread, 7, 26, 31
water-mill, 18, 19, 21
windmill, 21
wheat, 6, 9, 11-14
wheat germ, 9
wheat grain, 9, 14-17, 18, 21
wholemeal flour, 9
yeast, 7, 23

Now find out about:
Chocolate, Tea and Coffee,
The Potato
The Story of a Grain of Rice,
Milk
All About Salt
All About Sugar
other 'World of Food' titles available in the **Pocket Worlds** series.